AMERICAN HEROES

CESAR CHAVEZ

The Farm Workers'
Best Friend

AMERICAN HEROES

CESAR CHAVEZ
The Farm Workers'
Best Friend

SNEED B. COLLARD III

Marshall Cavendish
Benchmark
New York

To Geezer Mike, Kerry, and Olivia

Marshall Cavendish Benchmark
99 White Plains Road
Tarrytown, New York 10591
www.marshallcavendish.us

Library of Congress Cataloging-in-Publication Data
Collard, Sneed B.
Cesar Chavez : the farm workers' best friend / by Sneed B. Collard III.
p. cm. — (American heroes)
Includes index.
Summary: "A juvenile biography of Cesar Chavez, civil rights and labor
leader who founded the United Farm Workers union"—Provided by publisher.
ISBN 978-0-7614-4055-0
1. Chavez, Cesar, 1927-1993—Juvenile literature. 2. Labor leaders—United States—Biography—Juvenile literature.
3. Mexican American migrant agricultural laborers—Biography—Juvenile literature. I. Title.
HD6509.C48C646 2010
331.88′13092—dc22
[B]
2008034945

Editor: Joyce Stanton
Publisher: Michelle Bisson
Art Director: Anahid Hamparian
Series Designer: Anne Scatto
Printed in Malaysia
1 3 5 6 4 2

Images provided by Debbie Needleman, Picture Researcher, Portsmouth, NH, from the following sources:
Front cover: Arthur Schatz/Time & Life Pictures/Getty Images. *Back cover:* ©Franklin McMahon/CORBIS.
Pages i, 23: Arthur Schatz/Time & Life Pictures/Getty Images; *page ii:* ©Morton Beebe/CORBIS; *pages vi, 31:* Associated Press; *pages 1, 8, 20:* Walter P. Reuther Library, Wayne State University/Cesar E. Chavez Foundation; *pages 3, 11:* Cesar E. Chavez Foundation; *page 4:* Farm Security Administration, Office of War Information Photograph Collection, Library of Congress Prints and Photographs Division, Washington, D.C. (LC-USF34-019075-E); *page 7:* Farm Security Administration, Office of War Information Photograph Collection, Library of Congress Prints and Photographs Division, Washington, D.C. (LC-USF34-016425-C); *page 12:* ©Bettmann/CORBIS; *page 15:* St. Francis Gives His Coat to a Stranger.1296-97 (fresco) by Giotto di Bondone (c.1266-1337). San Francesco. Upper Church. Assisi, Italy/The Bridgeman Art Library; *pages 16,19:* ©Paul Fusco/Magnum Photos; *page 24:* ©Jim Sugar/CORBIS; *page 27:* ©Ted Streshinsky/CORBIS; *page 28:* Associated Press/Barry Sweet; *page 33:* Associated Press/Nick Ut; *page 34:* Associated Press/U.S. Postal Service; *page 41:* Blank Archives/Getty Images

CONTENTS

In the 1930s, farm workers in California struggled to survive.
Many farm workers still struggle today.

When Cesar Chavez was still a boy, his parents lost the family ranch. Without a home, the family had to move away to find work. They went to California, where they worked as farm laborers. They moved from one farm to another, picking different fruits and vegetables. It was back-breaking work for little money. Cesar and his siblings often went hungry. Many times, they slept in open fields. Those hard years would change Cesar's life forever. But many years later, Cesar would change the lives of other poor farm worker families.

Cesar Chavez was born on March 31, 1927, in Yuma, Arizona. "I had more happy moments as a child than unhappy moments," he remembered. He and his five brothers and sisters lived with their parents in the house of Cesar's grandmother. The house had no electricity or running water, but Cesar didn't mind. Every morning, he got up to help his father with farm chores. He and his brother Richard hunted rattlesnakes and played near the irrigation canal behind the house.

Cesar and his sister Rita at her first communion.
Although they lived simply, Cesar and his family shared many happy times.

The Great Depression forced Cesar's family—
and many others—to go to California to find work.

But the 1930s were the years of the Great Depression. Like most other Americans, Cesar's parents struggled to survive. Earlier, Cesar's father had been forced to sell his own land and business. When he couldn't pay the taxes on his mother's ranch, the state took that away, too. Soon, Cesar's family was forced to go to California to find work.

Cesar's family was not alone. During the Great Depression, hundreds of thousands of other people went to California. The only work most of them could find was picking fruit and vegetables for the owners of large farms, or growers as they were called. Life for these farm workers was awful. So many people needed jobs that growers could pay workers almost nothing for their labor. The growers also paid men called labor contractors. The labor contractors told workers about jobs they might find in different places. When the workers arrived, they often discovered that the jobs didn't exist or were much worse than promised.

Life for farm workers was hard. Many were lucky to have any shelter at all.

*By the eighth grade, Cesar had had enough of school
and the racism he faced there.*

During these years, Cesar and his sister attended thirty-eight different schools. "School was a nightmare," Cesar recalled. The teachers punished them for speaking Spanish. "There were lots of racist remarks that still hurt my ears."

Cesar finally quit school after the eighth grade. He joined his parents in the fields. Each morning, they would wake up at three or four o'clock and work for ten or twelve or fourteen hours. Sometimes, the entire family would earn only thirty cents a day.

Even with these hardships, Cesar's parents kept the family together. From his father, Cesar learned to work hard and respect himself. From his mother, he learned to help others, even when it was hard to do.

By the time he was seventeen, though, he had had enough of working in the fields. In 1944, during World War II, he joined the navy. He stayed in the navy for two years. Then, in 1948, he married a girl he had been dating for a long time. Her name was Helen Fabela.

Cesar and Helen got married after World War II.

*To support their growing family, Cesar and Helen moved all over California,
doing any work they could find.*

Like his parents, Cesar earned money by working in the fields. "We had a one-room shack without electricity or running water. It was bitterly cold," Cesar remembered. For the next several years, he and Helen moved from place to place, doing any work they could find. By now they also had children to support. Life seemed harder than ever. Then, Cesar met a priest named Father McDonnell.

Father McDonnell worked to solve the problems of poor people, especially farm workers. He began teaching Cesar about unfair laws that hurt poor people. He talked to Cesar about how rich growers kept farm workers poor. He gave Cesar books about people such as Gandhi and Saint Francis of Assisi who had worked for justice. Cesar had quit school a long time ago, but now, he began getting a real education.

Saint Francis of Assisi, who has a halo around his head in this painting, devoted himself to caring for the poor and sick. He also loved animals and nature.

*Unlike other workers, farm workers were not organized and had no power
to ask for better wages and working conditions.*

A big problem for farm workers was that they were not organized. Many other kinds of workers had already joined together in unions. A union gave workers power to ask for better wages, better working conditions, and health care. If an employer did not want to give workers these things, the union could call a strike. The workers would walk off the job until the employer agreed to give them better treatment. By the 1950s, workers in most industries belonged to unions. Farm workers did not.

Creating a farm workers' union was an especially difficult thing to do. Since workers moved around, going from one crop to another, they were hard to organize. And when workers did organize and go on strike, growers fired them and hired other workers, called scabs. Sometimes, growers beat up or even killed the people who went on strike. Workers feared the power and violence used by growers.

Workers and their families feared the power and violence of the growers.

Cesar believed that the best way to empower people was to encourage them to vote.

After meeting Father McDonnell, Cesar began learning how to organize people and give them power. For the next ten years, he traveled all over California. He helped Hispanics to vote. He helped striking workers. He fought against growers who hired illegal workers. But Cesar wanted to do more.

On September 30, 1962, Cesar and several other people started the National Farm Workers Association, or NFWA. This new union had no money and only a few members. But Cesar had a vision. He knew that if he talked to one person at a time, the union would grow.

From the beginning, the farm workers faced an uphill battle. Laws that protected other unions did not protect farm workers. Growers, courts, police, banks, grocery stores, and even railroads fought to keep the workers poor and powerless. Cesar didn't let this stop him. One worker at a time, he struggled to "grow" the union. Finally, the NFWA was ready to face the growers.

Cesar "grew" his union one person at a time.

In 1965, Cesar and the NFWA took on California's powerful grape growers.

In 1965, workers at a company that grew roses went on strike for better wages. The NFWA was able to help them. The union got the workers better pay, although it did not get them a contract that protected their jobs.

Later that year, the NFWA took on California's powerful grape growers. Grape workers were paid as little as one dollar an hour. They worked long days under the brutal sun. They breathed in dangerous poisons used to protect the grapes from pests.

Something had to be done.

All over California, grape workers walked off their jobs. In response, the growers brought in scabs. The growers got local police and judges to throw striking workers into jail. They even used another, corrupt union to beat up and threaten the grape workers. Cesar refused to use the "dirty" tactics that growers used. Instead, he and the union used only peaceful tools. They marched to tell people about their cause. To publicize their efforts, Cesar fasted, or stopped eating, for twenty-five days in a row. The union's most effective tool, however, was something called a boycott.

To let people know about their cause, hundreds of farm workers marched from Delano to Sacramento, California.

*The boycott of California grapes finally forced growers to
give farm workers better wages and working conditions.*

In the boycott, union workers went all over the country. They told grocery stores and other businesses about the terrible conditions grape workers faced. The workers asked businesses not to buy California grapes. The boycott worked. After a while, no one would buy California grapes and the growers began to lose money. Finally, after five long years, they were forced to sign contracts with the union. For the first time ever, grape workers had won basic rights that most other American workers already enjoyed.

Unfortunately, the struggles of farm workers were just beginning.

After winning contracts with the grape growers, the union faced fights with growers of lettuce and other crops. By this time, the NFWA had joined with another union to form the United Farm Workers of America, or UFW. Growers, other businesses, and even government agencies did everything they could to destroy this union. In 1975, however, Governor Jerry Brown helped pass the California Agricultural Labor Relations Act. This law protected the farm workers' right to organize into a union. It did not solve every problem, but it did make it easier for them to get fair treatment.

Finally, in 1975, workers got the right to organize.
Now they could proudly display their union label.

Today, farm workers all over the world keep struggling for fair pay and basic human rights. However, Cesar's own struggles ended when he died on April 23, 1993. During his life, he and Helen had never owned their own house. They had never earned more than $6,000 in a single year. But money was never important to Cesar. What was important was serving other people. His life reminds millions of poor people that the world can change for the better. With service and sacrifice, justice can be won.

Cesar's son Paul admires a stamp that honors his late father,
a man who lived to serve others.

Important Dates

1927 Born March 31 in Yuma, Arizona.

1937 His father loses the family ranch.

1939 Cesar's family members leave Arizona and begin living as migrant farm workers in California.

1944 Joins the United States Navy during World War II.

1948 Marries Helen Fabela.

1952 Begins actively working to help poor people.

1962 Starts the National Farm Workers Association union, or NFWA.

1965 NFWA supports farm workers' first strike against growers; also begins tackling grape growers.

1966 NFWA joins with another union to form the United Farm Workers union, or UFW.

1970 UFW signs first fair contracts for farm workers with California's grape growers.

1975 California passes the Agricultural Labor Relations Act, protecting farm workers' right to organize.

1993 Dies on April 23 in Yuma, Arizona, near where he was born.

Words to Know

boycott A plan by a group of people to refuse to buy a product or use a service in order to force a company to change its practices.

corrupt Bad; wicked.

Great Depression A time in America during the 1930s when many businesses failed and many people lost their jobs.

Hispanics People who have roots in Spain or the Spanish-speaking countries of America, including Mexico.

irrigation Supplying land with water, usually through canals or pipes, to grow crops.

justice Fair or right treatment.

labor contractors Men who find workers to perform a particular job. They are usually paid by an employer such as a grower. They also demand money from workers.

laborers People who do hard, physical work.

racist Having a belief that one group of people is better than another because of the color of their skin or their national heritage.

scab A person who takes the job of a worker who is on strike.

strike The stopping of work because of unfair conditions or low wages.

taxes Money that people must pay the government. Governments often charge people taxes on goods they buy, money they earn, or property they own.

union A group of workers joined together to protect their interests.

TO LEARN MORE ABOUT CESAR CHAVEZ

WEB SITES

The Cesar E. Chavez Foundation
   http://www.chavezfoundation.org/
The Fight in the Fields
   http://www.pbs.org/itvs/fightfields/cesarchavez.html
United Farm Workers
   http://www.ufw.org/

BOOKS

Cesar Chavez by Ginger Wadsworth. Lerner Publishing Group, 2005.

Cesar Chavez: A Hero for Everyone by Gary Soto. Simon & Schuster Children's Publishing, 2003.

César: ¡Sí, se puede! Yes, We Can! by Carmen T. Bernier-Grand. Marshall Cavendish Children's Books, 2004. (Also available in Spanish, © 2006.)

Harvesting Hope: The Story of Cesar Chavez by Kathleen Krull. Harcourt Children's Books, 2003.

PLACES TO VISIT

Memorials to Cesar Chavez are being created in many places. At the time of this writing, none are completed, but one under way is:

Cesar E. Chavez Memorial
Corner of Wolfskill and Truman Streets
San Fernando, CA
PHONE: (818) 898-1201
WEB SITE: **http://www.ci.san-fernando.ca.us/city_government/
departments/pubworks/current_projects/cesar_chavez/
dedication/index.shtml**

INDEX

Page numbers for illustrations are in boldface.

A Note on Quotes

ALL OF THE QUOTATIONS in this book have been taken from interviews contained in Jacques E. Levy's *Cesar Chavez: Autobiography of La Causa* (University of Minnesota Press, 2007). In most cases, I did not include the entire quotation, only the parts of sentences that were important for what I was trying to say.

—Sneed B. Collard III

ABOUT THE AUTHOR

SNEED B. COLLARD III is the author of more than fifty award-winning books for young people, including *Science Warriors*; *Wings*; *Pocket Babies*; and the four-book SCIENCE ADVENTURES series for Marshall Cavendish Benchmark. In addition to his writing, Sneed is a popular speaker and presents widely to students, teachers, and the general public. In 2006, he was selected as the Washington Post–Children's Book Guild Nonfiction Award winner for his achievements in children's writing. He is also the author of several novels for young adults, including *Dog Sense, Flash Point,* and *Double Eagle.* To learn more about Sneed, visit his Web site at www.sneedbcollardiii.com.